W9-BPM-573

AWESOME, DISGUSTING,

UNUSUAL FACTS ABOUT EVERYTHING

STINKY, SQUISHY, AND SLIMY

Eric Braun

BLACK
RABBIT
BOOKS

Hi Jinx is published by Black Rabbit Books
P.O. Box 3263, Mankato, Minnesota, 56002.
www.blackrabbitbooks.com
Copyright © 2019 Black Rabbit Books

Marysa Storm, editor; Michael Sellner, designer;
Catherine Cates, production designer;
Omay Ayres, photo researcher

Library of Congress Cataloging-in-Publication Data
Names: Braun, Eric, 1971- author.
Title: Awesome, disgusting, unusual facts about everything stinky,
squishy, and slimy / by Eric Braun.
Description: Mankato, Minnesota : Black Rabbit Books, [2019] |
Series: Hi jinx. Our gross, awesome world | Includes bibliographical
references and index.
Identifiers: LCCN 2017045560 (print) | LCCN 2018000579 (ebook) |
ISBN 9781680726169 (e-book) | ISBN 9781680726107 (library binding) |
ISBN 9781680727524 (paperback)
Subjects: LCSH: Odors–Juvenile literature. | Smell–Juvenile literature. |
Curiosities and wonders–Juvenile literature. | Touch–Juvenile
literature. Classification: LCC QP458 (ebook) |
LCC QP458 .B73 2018 (print) | DDC 612.8/6–dc23
LC record available at https://lccn.loc.gov/2017045560

Printed in the United States. 4/18

Image Credits

Alamy: Brandon Cole Marine Photography, 8 (top);
cbimages, 3, 8 (bttm); John Cancalosi, 11 (lizard);
Dreamstime: Lukas Blazek, 6 (bird); imgur.com: EXPOOKA,
9; Shutterstock: advent 17; Albert Ziganshin, 4 (monsters),
5; anfisa focusova, 15 (bkgd); Angeliki Vel, 10–11 (grass); AN
Photographer2463, 6 (poop); blambca, 12 (ill. gum), 16 (people);
David Litman, 12 (bkgd); Eric Broder Van Dyke, 15 (lake); Fabio
Berti, 19; frescomovie, 7 (bkgd); Jarun Ontakrai, 20 (bacteria); Jon
Larter, 13 (clothespin, fumes); Julien Tromeur, 2–3, 21 (germ); Laura
Dinraths, Cover (sea cucumber); Lightspring, 18 (tongue); Magnia,
16 (bkgd), 21 (bkgd); Nathapol Kongseang, 10–11 (bat); opicobello,
13 (torn paper); Pasko Maksim, Back Cover (torn paper), 10 (bttm),
19 (top), 23 (top), 24; Paul Marcus, 15 (flower); Peter Fodor, 7 (poo
ball); Pitju, 8 (corner), 21 (corner); PongMoji, 4 (bkgd); ridjam,
7 (beetle); Ron Dale, Cover (marker stroke), 1 (marker stroke), 3
(top), 5 (top), 6 (top), 13 (top), 16 (top), 20 (top);
Sarawut Padungkwan, 12 (guy), 15 (roaches);
Sebastian Kaulitzki, 18 (tooth, germs), 23 (germ);
Sergey Uryadnikov, 13 (seal); Sunflowerr, 1 (bkgd);
SoulArtimage, 6–7 (poo, foot); SvedOliver, 15(pool);
Tony Oshlick, 6–7 (flies, fumes); totallypic, 20 (arrow); Tueris,
18 (blue); your, 11 (clouds)Every effort has been made to contact
copyright holders for material reproduced in this book. Any
omissions will be rectified in subsequent printings if notice
is given to the publisher.

CONTENTS

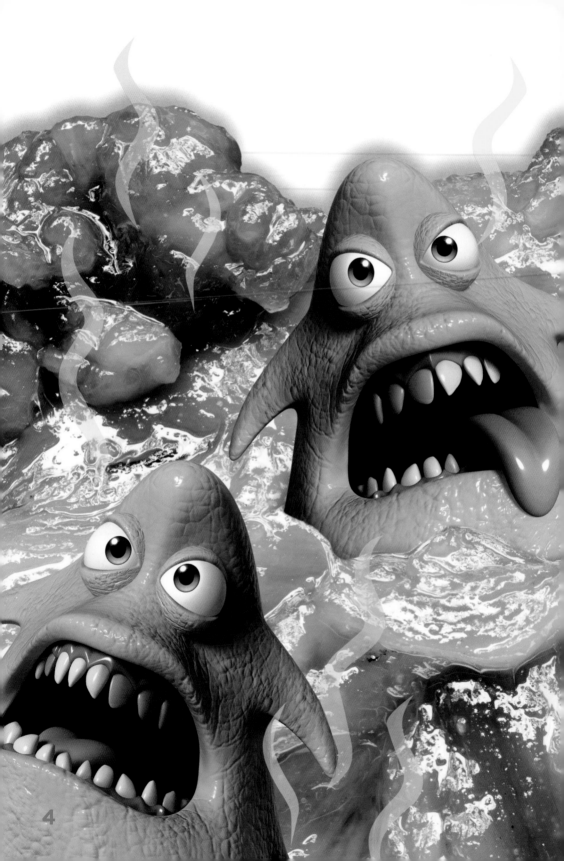

Chapter 1

READY TO GET GROSSED OUT?

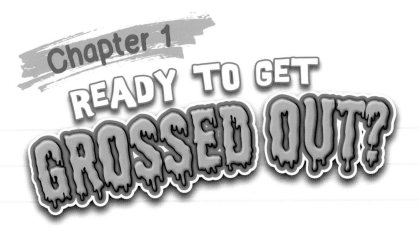

Phew! Something stinks! Maybe it's all the squishy, slimy stuff in this book. There's a lot of it.

Some animals do the grossest things. Some places are rotten and **rank**. Even people are pretty nasty. Read on to learn all about snot, slime, and other awesome things.

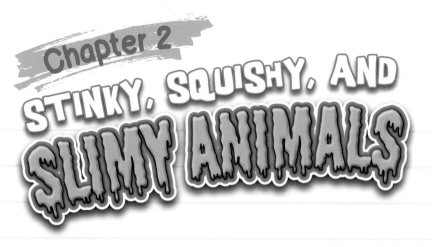

Chapter 2
STINKY, SQUISHY, AND SLIMY ANIMALS

Elephants eat a lot. That means they poop a lot too! An elephant produces more than 100 pounds (45 kilograms) of poop a day.

On hot days, you might go to the pool. Turkey vultures, on the other hand, poop on their feet. It helps cool them off.

Elephant poop can be made into paper.

hagfish

sea cucumber

The fulmar chicks' vomit oil makes their enemies' feathers stick together. Then they can't fly away.

Slimy Self-Defense

The hagfish might be the world's slimiest animal. Sticky slime drips out of **glands** on its sides. The slime covers the fish's body. The slippery goo makes it hard for **predators** to grab the creature.

Some sea cucumbers have a gross way of protecting themselves. When threatened, they poop out part of their **organs**. Their missing body parts grow back.

Bigger birds try to eat fulmar chicks. To defend themselves, the chicks vomit an orange oil on predators. The slimy oil smells like rotten fish. Yum!

Blood

Vampire bats live on blood. Sometimes they can't find enough blood to drink. But that's OK. Other vampire bats help out. They throw up blood for others to drink.

Some vampire bats can double their weight with one night of drinking blood.

When threatened by predators, horned lizards squirt blood from their eyes. The blood confuses predators.

Chapter 3

STINKY, SQUISHY, AND SLIMY PLACES

There are some pretty interesting places you can visit.

California's Bubblegum Alley has a squishy **tradition**. People stick used gum to the walls.

More than 60,000 seals live on Seal Island in South Africa. They poop all over the rocky land. That makes for one squishy and stinky island.

Smelly Spots

Salty water and dead shrimp fill Utah's Great Salt Lake. Together, they make a smell that's not so great.

Sumatra, a tropical island, can be a smelly place. The island's **corpse** flower rarely blooms. But when it does, it smells like dead bodies.

Another stinky place is found in Iceland. The Blue Lagoon has many **geothermal** pools. They smell like rotten eggs. But people still pay to soak in the relaxing hot water.

Great Salt Lake

corpse flower

geothermal pool

15

Chapter 4
THE STINKY, SQUISHY, AND SLIMY HUMAN BODY

Your body can be pretty gross too. Most people's noses make about 2 gallons (8 liters) of snot each week. You swallow about ¼ gallon (1 l) each day.

Speaking of noses, you might want to plug yours. The average person farts about 15 times a day.

You better cover your cough too. Coughs can reach speeds of more than 50 miles (80 kilometers) per hour. Gross germs can travel far at those speeds.

Your snot is about 95 percent water.

Guts and Bacteria

You have a lot of guts! No, really! Small intestines are about 20 feet (6 meters) long all stretched out. Large intestines reach about 5 feet (2 m) long when stretched out.

Your body is full of tiny living things known as bacteria. They live on your teeth. They call your tongue home. They're in your guts and poop too.

About 100 trillion bacteria live in a person's gut.

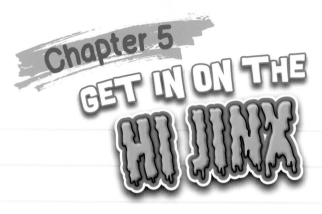

Chapter 5
GET IN ON THE
HI JINX

Bacteria may be gross, but some are good for you. You wouldn't be able to survive without them.

One scientist wanted to learn more about bacteria. So she asked people to bring her their poop. She studied the poop's bacteria. But that's not the weird part. She put the bacteria in dishes with special dye. Bacteria **activated** the dye. When the bacteria grew, artwork bloomed in the dishes. There are many gross things that may be helpful. Some are even beautiful!

Take It One Step More

1. Most bacteria help people. But many people think they're gross or bad. Why do you think that is?

2. Pick a place from Chapter 3 to visit. Why would you go there?

3. Some animals defend themselves in gross ways. Why might that be?

GLOSSARY

activate (AK-tuh-veyt)—to start working
or cause to start working

corpse (KORPS)—a dead body

geothermal (jee-oh-THUR-muhl)—of,
relating to, or using the natural heat produced
inside Earth

gland (GLAND)—a body part that produces
a substance to be used by the body or given
off from it

organ (OHR-guhn)—a bodily structure
consisting of cells and tissues that performs
a specific function

predator (PRED-uh-tuhr)—an animal that
eats other animals

rank (RANGK)—having a strong,
unpleasant smell

tradition (truh-DISH-uhn)—a belief or
custom handed down from one generation
to another

BOOKS

Chigna, Charles. *Animal Planet Strange Unusual Gross and Cool Animals.* New York: Time Inc. Books, 2016.

Perish, Patrick. *Disgusting Animals.* Totally Disgusting. Minneapolis: Bellwether Media, 2014.

Weird but True: Human Body: 300 Outrageous Facts about Your Awesome Anatomy. National Geographic Kids. Washington, D.C.: National Geographic, 2017.

WEBSITES

13 Facts to Gross Out Your Parents
kids.nationalgeographic.com/explore/13-facts-to-gross-out-your-parents/

Fun Facts and Trivia
kids.niehs.nih.gov/games/riddles/jokes/fun-facts-and-trivia/index.htm

Funny Science Facts
www.sciencekids.co.nz/sciencefacts/funny.html

INDEX